HAITIAN CREOLE CHIDLREN'S BOOK

COLORS AND SHAPES

FOR YOUR KIDS

AUTHOR
ROAN WHITE

ILLUSTRATIONS
FEDERICO BONIFACINI

ROUJ

BLE

JÒN

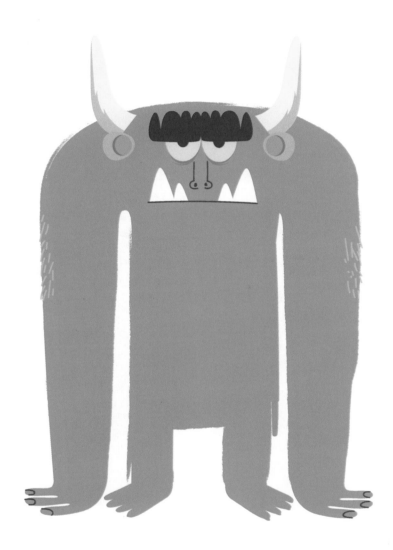

VÈ

ORANJ

MOV

NWA

MARON

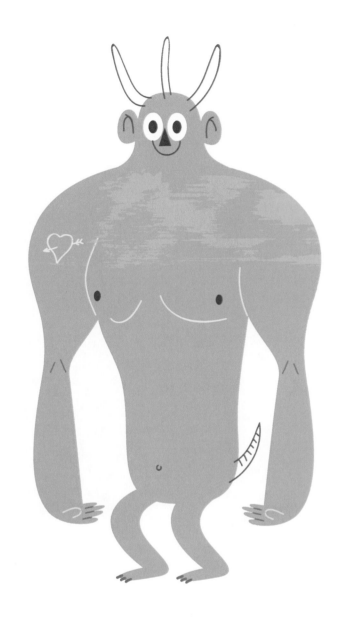

ROZ

GRIS

TRIYANG

WONN

KARE

REKTANG

LOZANJ

PARALELOGRAM

TRAPÈZ

DYAMAN

PENTAGÒN

EGZAGÒN

OKTAGÒN

CPSIA information can be obtained
at www.ICGtesting.com
Printed in the USA
BVRC101941290421
606155BV00001B/10